The Bread of Life

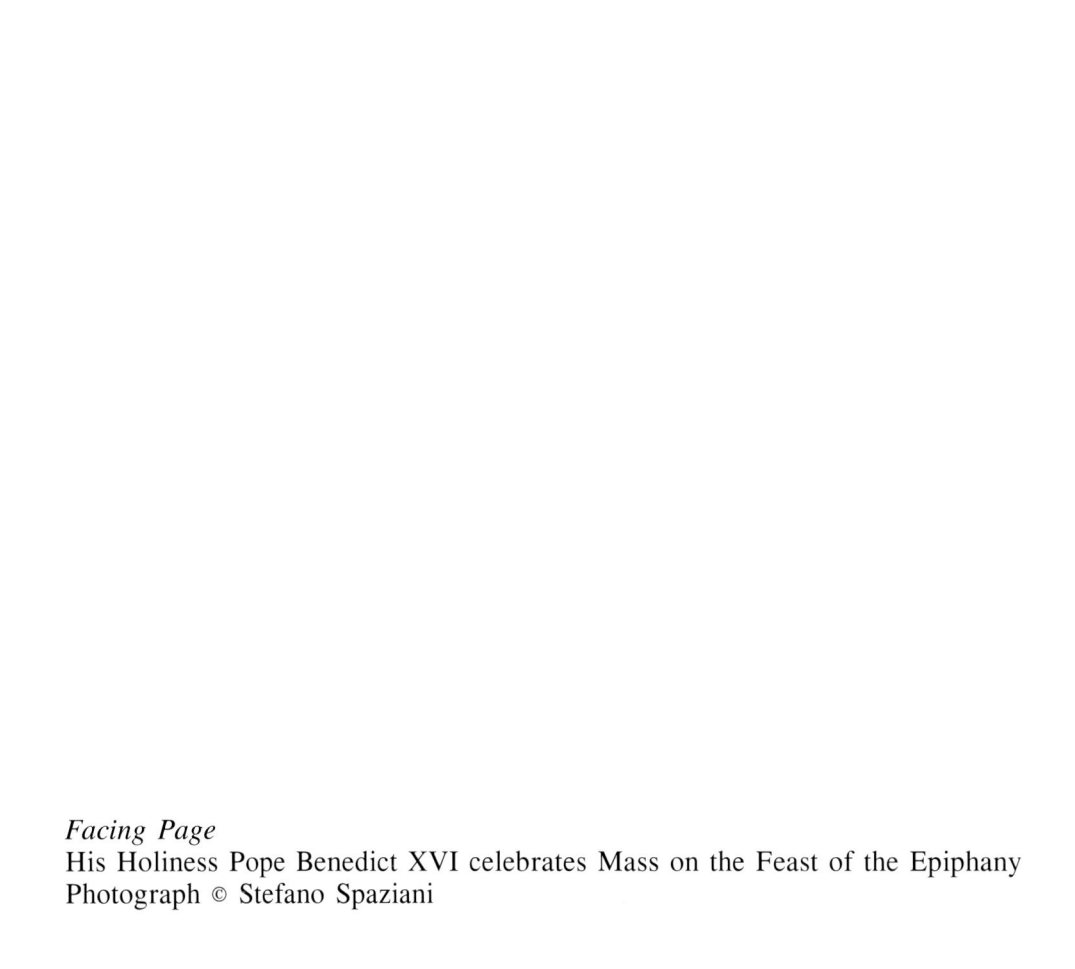

Facing Page
His Holiness Pope Benedict XVI celebrates Mass on the Feast of the Epiphany
Photograph © Stefano Spaziani

THE BREAD OF LIFE

A Preparation Course for First Confession and First Communion

This book belongs to..

who received Jesus, the Bread of Life

in First Holy Communion on ....

The Bread of Life

Preparing for First Confession and First Communion

Father Martin Edwards

Artwork by David Clayton

Photographs by Wayne Perry

GRACEWING

First published in 2007

Gracewing
2 Southern Avenue, Leominster
Herefordshire
HR6 0QF

Published in Australia by
Freedom Publishing Company Ltd
582 Queensberry Street
North Melbourne Victoria 3051
Australia

All rights reserved. No part of this publication may be reproduced, stored in a retrieval system, or transmitted in any form, or by any means, electronic, mechanical, photocopying, recording or otherwise, without the written permission of the publisher.

Text © Martin Edwards 2007
Artwork © David Clayton 2007
Photographs © Wayne Perry 2007

None of the images from this book may be reproduced without written permission from the artist or the photographer.

NB the photograph on page 32 of a girl going to Confession portrays a confessional equipped with a glass-fronted door.

The right of Martin Edwards to be identified as the author of this work has been asserted in accordance with the Copyright, Designs and Patents Act 1988

ISBN 0 85244 121 5
978 0 85244 121 3

Typesetting by Action Publishing Technology Ltd,
Gloucester, GL1 5SR

Printed in Italy by
Grafiche Flaminia Srl

CONTENTS

FOREWORD *by The Very Reverend Ignatius Harrison, Cong.Orat., Provost of the London Oratory of Saint Philip Neri*   ix

FOR PARENTS AND TEACHERS   1

1.	GOD THE CREATOR OF ALL	5
2.	SIN COMES INTO THE WORLD	9
3.	GOD SENDS US HIS SON	13
4.	BAPTISM — A NEW BEGINNING	17
5.	THE TEN COMMANDMENTS	21
6.	THE PRODIGAL SON	25
7.	THE GOOD SHEPHERD	29
8.	MEETING JESUS IN CONFESSION	33
9.	HOW TO GO TO CONFESSION	36
10.	THE BREAD OF LIFE	39
11.	THE SACRIFICE OF JESUS	43
12.	JESUS — GOD WITH US	47
13.	JESUS — OUR SAVIOUR AND OUR GUEST	51
14.	JESUS IS VERY NEAR	55
15.	IT IS RIGHT TO GIVE HIM THANKS	59

PRAYERS   63

GLOSSARY OF KEY WORDS   64

Nihil Obstat: The Reverend Canon John Redford STL LSS DD

Imprimatur: The Reverend Monsignor Richard Moth MA JCL KCHS VG
Archdiocese of Southwark
20th June 2007

The Nihil Obstat and Imprimatur are a declaration that a publication is considered to be free from doctrinal or moral error. It is not implied that those who have granted the Nihil Obstat and Imprimatur agree with the contents, opinions or statements expressed.

FOREWORD

The Very Reverend Ignatius Harrison, Cong.Orat.
Provost of the London Oratory of Saint Philip Neri

One of the most important things we Catholics can ever do is to hand on the sublime truths of our divine Catholic faith to our children, the future generation of the Church Christ founded. Parents, priests, catechists – we all have a most serious responsibility to do everything in our power to ensure that our children are well instructed, both in the doctrinal content and in the actual practice of our holy religion. This is particularly crucial in the way we help children to prepare for the reception of the Sacrament of Penance, their first confession, and then their reception for the first time of the most Blessed Sacrament of the altar – their first Holy Communion.

Sadly, some of the catechetical material produced in the last few decades has been lamentably inadequate for this necessary task. That is why we should be so grateful for the publication of *The Bread of Life*. There has long been a real pastoral need for a preparation course like this: orthodox, pious (in the true sense) and practical – fully Catholic. It will be a valuable resource in any home, parish and school that wishes to impart the fullness of the faith to their children who are preparing for these two life-changing sacraments.

The living tradition of God's Holy Church is maintained by two elements: the life-giving breath of the Holy Spirit, the Soul of the Church, and our own human efforts, the work of human hands. *The Bread of Life* is a splendid work, and will undoubtedly serve as a valuable instrument which the Holy Spirit can use for His own good purposes: to teach our children true sorrow for their sins, sincere repentance, amendment of life, and above all, an abiding love of the Real Presence of Our Lord Jesus Christ in the adorable sacrament of His love – in short – the life of grace.

Ignatius Harrison, C.O.

FOR PARENTS AND TEACHERS

The Bread of Life is designed to prepare children for the Sacraments of Penance and First Holy Communion following a course of fifteen lessons. The material is aimed at children of about eight years of age, but it may, of course, when suitably modified, be used by children both younger and older.

Each lesson begins with either a specially commissioned icon or a photograph. These are an integral part of each lesson, and the text often refers to elements found in the pictures. The text for each chapter introduces the child to several key concepts which are repeated at the end as 'Key Words'. A glossary at the end of the book gives a simple definition of each key word, but children should be encouraged to discover the meaning of each word from the written text, and should be quizzed from time to time to check that they have understood these key concepts.

Each chapter concludes with a 'reinforcement' activity. Sometimes this is simply a question of filling in the letters of missing words (again, to be discovered by reviewing the text); at other times the children are asked to draw or paint a picture or compose prayers. The book concludes with prayers a child should know before making his First Holy Communion. These prayers could be used at the start and end of each lesson.

The scope of this book is limited: to prepare a child for Confession and Holy Communion. Important areas of Christian doctrine will, inevitably, be missing – this work lays no claim to being a comprehensive catechism. The Decree *Quem singulari* of the Congregation on the Sacraments (8 August 1910), by which children who had not yet been confirmed were first admitted to Holy Communion, states that 'For first confession and for first communion a full and perfect knowledge of Christian doctrine is not necessary.' However this same decree also teaches that 'The knowledge of religion which is required in a child, that he may prepare himself fittingly for his first communion is that … he distinguishes Eucharistic bread from common and corporeal, in order that he may approach the most Blessed Eucharist with that devotion which his age carries.'

It is hoped that a child following this course of preparation will be able to make this vital distinction between Jesus the Bread of Life and ordinary bread, and approach the Blessed Sacrament devoutly and reverently, and to discover the 'Eucharistic amazement' of which the late Holy Father Pope John Paul II spoke so movingly in *Ecclesia de Eucharistia*, the mystery that lies at the heart of the Christian life.

The Bread of Life

1. GOD THE CREATOR OF ALL

In the beginning God created Heaven and earth.

These are the very first words in the Holy Bible: *In the beginning God created Heaven and earth.* The first pages of the Bible tell us how God our loving Father made everything; as we say at Mass in the prayer called the *Creed*, God is the maker of all things visible and invisible. This means that God made everything that we can see, even those things that are so small or so far away that we need a microscope or telescope to see them. He also made the things we cannot see even with a telescope or a microscope: for example, the angels who serve and praise Him in Heaven, or the guardian angels who watch over each one of us.

God made everything: He is the Creator, and all things are His creatures. To *create* means to make things out of nothing. When we make something, we use other things to make it. An artist uses paints to make a picture, a cook uses food to make a meal. God alone can make things out of nothing; He creates with a word, with a command. Ask your parents or your teacher to read the first pages of the Bible with you. There, in the Book of Genesis, the first book of the Holy Bible, you will find the story of creation. Firstly God said: 'Let there be light!' and there was light. Then He created the Heavens, the earth, the sun and the moon and all the stars; then He filled this earth with all the wonderful plants and flowers, trees, animals, fish and birds. He made these things for us: for us to use and care for, and we should always thank Him for all that He has given us. The Bible tells us that God saw that all these things were good: of course they were, since they were made by God who is goodness itself! Nothing that God makes is bad, although people sometimes use His good things badly. The picture for this lesson shows God creating and filling the earth. But no human being saw this, since God created man last of all.

He kept the best until last. Adam and Eve, the first people, lived in the Garden of Eden. They were the last and most important things God made on earth: the Bible tells us that God saw that they were *very* good. They were not only very good but very happy as well: God loved them, and they loved God. He spoke to them, and they always listened to His voice, and did what He commanded them. Adam and Eve lived in the Garden of Eden as God's friends; the life and love of God, which we call His holy grace, was with them always. It is God's grace that makes us truly happy, and Adam and Eve lived in His grace with the whole world before them to care for and enjoy.

KEY WORDS FOR CHAPTER 1

(NOTE for parents and teachers: the meanings of these words, and those found at the end of subsequent chapters, will be found on page 64)

Genesis
Angel
Creator
Creature
Adam and Eve
Grace

Fill in the blanks

The first three words of the Holy Bible are I _ _ t _ _ b _ _ _ _ _ _ _ _.

The first book of the Holy Bible is called the Book of G _ _ _ _ _ _.

The first people God created were called A _ _ _ and E _ _.

In the box below write down the names of three things God created.

In this box write the names of three things you have made, and what you used to make them.

God has given all of us a guardian angel. We cannot see our angel, but he sees and loves us. Imagine what your guardian angel looks like and draw a picture of him.

Prayer to our Guardian Angel

Angel of God, my guardian dear
To whom God's love commits me here,
Ever this day be at my side
To light and guard, to rule and guide. Amen.

2. SIN COMES INTO THE WORLD

The picture for this lesson shows the beautiful Garden of Eden where Adam and Eve lived, but it is not a happy picture. Adam and Eve are leaving the garden and look sad and frightened; the animals are attacking each other, and an unusual and crafty-looking snake is coiled around a very special tree. What has happened to turn God's beautiful world into a place of sadness and suffering? The answer to this is a little but terrible word: *sin*. Adam and Eve have committed the first sin, the original sin, and with that sin, death, sadness and suffering have come into our world.

How did it happen? When God made the world and the first human beings, someone was jealous of their happiness. That person was the devil, who had once been the greatest of the angels of God, but had turned against God. The devil knew that it was no good attacking God, since God is all-powerful, so he decided to try to make God suffer by spoiling His creation.

God had given Adam and Eve a marvellous place to live in, and the whole world to serve their needs. He told them that they could eat the fruit of all the trees in the garden except one: they were not to eat the fruit of the tree of the knowledge of good and evil. And He warned them that if they did eat the fruit of that tree, then they would die. God gave the first human beings the gift of free will, which meant that they could freely choose to love Him and obey Him, and they could also freely choose to turn away from Him and disobey Him. So the devil tempted them to disobey God, and to eat the fruit He had told them never to touch. They listened to the devil, and ate the fruit. They turned against God, they disobeyed him. Sin had come into the world: the first sin we call original sin. This sad event is called the Fall since, by sin, our first parents fell away from grace and happiness and God's friendship into the sorrow of sin.

When Adam and Eve turned against God, they lost the life of God, His holy grace in their souls. With sin comes sadness and fear and suffering. To sin is to disobey God our loving Father by refusing to do what He has told us. All sin causes the suffering and sadness Adam and Eve discovered when they disobeyed God. They now had to leave the Garden of Eden, and make their living with difficulty in a world which was no longer the paradise God had made. Worse still, since they were the parents of all human beings all their children, the whole human race, would be born suffering from original sin.

They had turned against God, but God never stopped loving them. He promised them a Saviour; He brightened the sadness of sin with the hope that one day He would send His Son, Jesus Christ our Lord who would restore the human race to God's friendship and bring back grace to our souls.

KEY WORDS FOR CHAPTER 2

Sin
Free Will
Original Sin
Devil
Saviour

Fill in the blanks

Adam and Eve were tempted by the d _ _ _ _ ; they listened to him and d _ _ _ _ _ _ _ _ the command of God.

This first sin is called o _ _ _ _ _ _ _ s _ _ .

Through this sin they lost the life of God, His holy g _ _ _ _ in their souls; but God promised to send them a S _ _ _ _ _ _ _ .

Draw a picture of the tree of the knowledge of good and evil. If you like you can add drawings of Adam and Eve.

3. GOD SENDS US HIS SON

Many years had passed since Adam and Eve first disobeyed God and lost his grace. Over the centuries sin increased, and people forgot about God their loving Father and worshipped false gods. But God helped one people to know and love Him: the Jewish people from which the Saviour would be born.

Every Christmas we hear again the wonderful story of our Saviour's birth. We remember how God sent the angel Gabriel to the town of Nazareth in Palestine which we rightly call the Holy Land, to visit Mary, a girl He had specially prepared to be the mother of His only Son. The angel Gabriel greeted Mary with the words we repeat every time we say *Hail Mary, full of grace, the Lord is with thee!* He asked her if she would be the mother of Jesus. Mary said *Yes*, and, at that moment, the Son of God began to live on earth, hidden inside His mother Mary. God was the Father of Jesus Christ, and God found His Son a foster father to look after the child Jesus and His mother Mary. He was Joseph, a carpenter, who married Mary and became the father of the Holy Family.

Nine months later Jesus was born, but not in Nazareth where Mary and Joseph lived. In those days the Romans ruled the Holy Land and many other countries as well. Caesar Augustus, the emperor of Rome, gave an order that a census of the whole empire should be taken, that is, a great list of all the people who were his subjects. This was the first time that this had been done, and everyone had to go to his own town to be registered and entered on the great list that would be sent to Rome. Now, since Joseph came from Bethlehem in Judea in the south of the Holy Land, it was to Bethlehem that Joseph and Mary his wife had to go to be registered. It was a difficult journey since Mary was just about to give birth to Jesus, but they had to obey the orders of their Roman rulers.

When they got to Bethlehem they found the town full of people who, like them, were there on account of the census. All the inns were full, and Mary and Joseph could find nowhere to stay. In the end they found lodging in a stable. And so it was that the Son of God was born in a barn, and since, of course, there were no beds there, He slept in a manger, a trough from which the animals took their food.

Who was there to witness the birth of the Saviour the world had waited for since the Fall? Only His mother Mary, St Joseph and the animals who lived in that stable! The angels of God also saw the birth of Jesus, and these angels told some shepherds who were nearby the glorious news that the Saviour had been born. The angels were full of joy at the birth of Jesus, and, in the skies above Bethlehem on the first Christmas night they sang a song that we hear most Sundays at Mass: it was the first *Gloria – Glory to God in the highest; and on earth peace to men of good will.*

It is right that we should hear the *Gloria* and remember that first Christmas night when we come to Mass because, in the Holy Mass, as at Bethlehem, Jesus our Saviour comes to be with us. In the Mass as at Bethlehem two thousand years ago He is hidden, so that only His friends know that He is there. On Christmas night the shepherds saw a new-born baby, but God had sent His angels to tell them that this tiny infant was their Saviour. At the most important part of the Mass we see what we call the *Host*, lifted up by the priest: it looks like a tiny piece of bread, but we know that this is our Saviour and our God. Like those shepherds we are called to come and adore our Saviour when we go to Mass. *Glory to God in the highest! Come, let us adore Him!*

KEY WORDS FOR CHAPTER 3

Nazareth
Foster father
Census
Bethlehem
Adore
Gloria
Host

Fill in the blanks

M _ _ _ is the mother of Jesus.

God gave Jesus a foster father called J _ _ _ _ _.

Jesus was born in the city of B _ _ _ _ _ _ _ _.

When Jesus was born, angels appeared to some s _ _ _ _ _ _ _ _ who were watching over their flocks; they told them that the Saviour was born and sang G _ _ _ _ to God in the h _ _ _ _ _ _.

Think about your last Christmas. What did you do then? What presents did you give and receive? Write a prayer to thank God for the great gift of His Son Jesus, and for the many gifts you have been given by Him and by people who love you. You could say this prayer to Him next time you go to Mass.

4. BAPTISM — A NEW BEGINNING

For thirty years Jesus lived in Nazareth, working as a carpenter, and known only to His family, friends and neighbours. His public work began with His baptism when He was about thirty years old. His cousin John the Baptist was baptising people in the river Jordan, and Jesus joined the crowds there. When John saw Jesus, he recognised Him at once, and did not want to baptise the Lord. But Jesus insisted, and the picture for today's lesson shows what happened next. As John poured the water over Jesus, the heavens opened, and the Holy Spirit, appearing as a dove, came to rest over Jesus, and from Heaven the voice of God the Father was heard saying: *You are my beloved Son; with you I am well pleased.*

You probably do not remember the day of your baptism, since most people are baptised as babies. We are baptised so that our sins can be washed away and we can become children of God and members of His holy Catholic Church. Jesus did not have to be baptised since He had no sins and was already the Son of God, but He chose to give us an example, and He ordered His disciples, with His last words on earth, to go and baptise all people. His disciples, and the men the disciples selected to carry on this work, have been obeying that order now for nearly two thousand years. When a baby comes for baptism he has, of course, committed no sins himself – a baby is too young to do that. But we are all born with original sin, the sin committed by our first parents Adam and Eve, and this needs to be washed away.

Why is water used for baptism? Well, water washes and makes things clean, and it also does something even more important – it gives life. We could live without washing (although that would not be very nice) but we cannot live more than a day or two without something to drink. The waters of baptism wash away the stains of sin and give us the life of God, His holy grace. When we were baptised the priest poured water over us while saying *I baptise you in the name of the Father, and of the Son, and of the Holy Spirit.* It was Jesus who taught us to do this, and told us what words we must use.

Father, Son and Holy Spirit: these are the three Persons of the Most Blessed Trinity. There is only one God, but in God there are three Persons. Not three gods, but three Persons in one God. When Jesus was baptised the Holy Trinity was made known: the voice of God the Father came from Heaven, Jesus was seen on the earth, and the Holy Spirit appeared as a dove. We are baptised in the name of the Holy Trinity, and through baptism the Holy Trinity make their home in us.

When Jesus was baptised God said *You are my beloved Son; in you I am well pleased.* When we were baptised and sin was washed away and grace given to us, we too became the beloved children of God. We should pray that God our loving Father will always be pleased with us.

KEY WORDS FOR CHAPTER 4

Baptism
River Jordan
John the Baptist
Catholic Church
Blessed Trinity

Fill in the blanks

The three Persons of the Holy Trinity are:

God the F _ _ _ _ _

God the S _ _

God the H _ _ _ S _ _ _ _ _ _.

God the Father, God the Son and God the Holy Spirit are the three Persons of the Most Blessed T _ _ _ _ _ _.

There is only one God, but in God there are three P _ _ _ _ _ _.

In the box below, draw and colour a picture of your baptism. Write down the names of any people you know where there (parents, godparents, priest, brothers and sisters).

When you were baptised, the priest poured water over you and said *I baptise you in the name of the Father, and of the Son, and of the Holy Spirit.* Ask members of your family about your baptism and try to fill in this form.

I was baptised in the Church of ....

The date of my baptism was ....

My godparents were ....

The name of the priest who baptised me is ....

5. THE TEN COMMANDMENTS

To please God we have to live in His grace, and to help us do that He has given us a set of rules called the Ten Commandments. The picture shows Moses and the stone tablets on which God wrote the Ten Commandments. Moses had been chosen by God to lead His people from slavery in Egypt to a land He promised them where they would be happy and free. The way to that promised land led through a desert, and for forty years God cared for His people as they made their way slowly through the wilderness, sending them a special bread from Heaven called *Manna* and finding fresh water for them to drink.

Even though God had freed them from slavery and guided and looked after them, His people often sinned and rebelled against Him. So God sent them the Ten Commandments to help them to be good and happy. God wrote the Commandments on two great pieces of stone, and told his faithful servant Moses, the leader of the Jews, to make His Commandments known to them. Here are the Ten Commandments:

The Ten Commandments

1. Hear, O Israel, I am the Lord your God; you shall not have other gods before me.
2. You shall not take God's name in vain.
3. Remember to keep the Lord's day holy.
4. Honour your father and your mother.
5. You shall not kill.
6. You shall not commit adultery.
7. You shall not steal.
8. You shall not lie.
9. You shall not covet your neighbour's wife.
10. You shall not covet your neighbour's goods.

Even though these rules were given by God to his people well over three thousand years ago, they will still help us now to live as God's children if we love and obey Him by keeping them. The first three commandments tell us how to love and honour God, and the next seven tell us how to love and serve others.

If we want to please God and be happy with Him now and forever in Heaven, we must always honour and keep the commandments He has given us.

KEY WORDS FOR CHAPTER 5

Manna
The Ten Commandments
Moses
The Lord's Day
Covet

Fill in the blanks

God gave His people the T _ _ C _ _ _ _ _ _ _ _ _ _. He also fed them in the desert with bread from Heaven called M _ _ _ _.

M _ _ _ _ was the man who led God's people out of Egypt through the desert to the promised land.

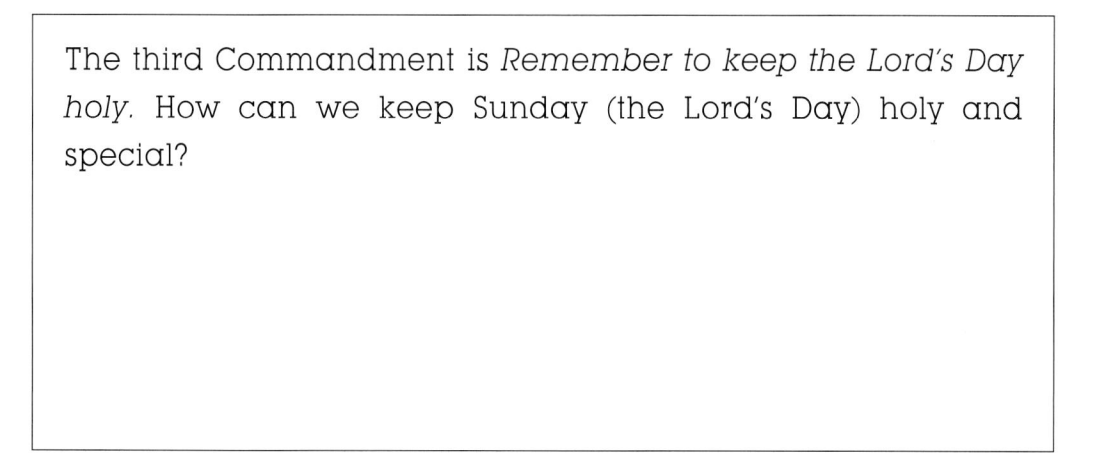

The third Commandment is *Remember to keep the Lord's Day holy.* How can we keep Sunday (the Lord's Day) holy and special?

The fourth Commandment is *Honour your father and your mother.* In what ways can we honour our parents?

6. THE PRODIGAL SON

When Jesus had to teach people an important lesson, He often used to tell them a *parable*. A parable is an interesting story that contains an important truth. We easily remember an interesting story, and so, almost without knowing it, we learn an important lesson.

One of the most famous parables of Jesus is the parable of the Prodigal Son (*prodigal* is another way of saying *wasteful* or *extravagant*). You will find this parable in the fifteenth chapter of Saint Luke's Gospel. It is the story of a young man who wants to escape from his father, and to do so he demands his inheritance, that is, the share of his father's property and money that would come to him when his father died. By asking for his inheritance the son was telling his father that, as far as he was concerned, he was already dead and buried. His father gave it to him and he went off far away and began to waste all the money he had been given. Before too long all the money was gone, and the young man began to starve. He had to get a job looking after pigs, and he was so hungry that he would have eaten the pigs' food himself, but no one gave him any.

It was only then that he came to his senses. He realised that even his father's servants had enough to eat, while he was starving to death. So he decided to go back to his father's house: he would tell his father that he had sinned against him and against God – he was no longer fit to be called his son, but perhaps he could become one of his servants. And so he started off home.

Now, while he was still a long way from home, his father saw him. He had been watching and waiting for him! His son began to tell him how sorry he was, but his father interrupted him. The father welcomed his son, as you can see in the picture for this lesson: he forgave him the great wrong he had done. He made him his son again, and began rejoicing and celebrating the return of the prodigal son.

What lesson does this beautiful parable teach us? It tells us about sin and forgiveness. When we sin, we turn away from God and His Commandments, just as the boy turned away from his father. When we sin we move away from God, just as the boy went off into a far away country. Sin makes us unhappy, just as the prodigal son became miserable. But this unhappiness, the knowledge that we have done wrong, can help us turn back to God, just as the prodigal son returned to his father.

The father in the parable welcomed and forgave his son, and, in the same way, God our loving Father always welcomes and forgives sinners who turn back to Him. The father rejoiced when his son came back: Jesus tells us that the angels in Heaven rejoice when a sinner turns to God. The beautiful parable of the prodigal son teaches us that God never stops loving us, and that even if we turn away from Him He will always welcome us if we are truly sorry and come back to Him.

KEY WORDS FOR CHAPTER 6

Parable
Prodigal
Inheritance

Fill in the blanks

When we sin we t _ _ _ a _ _ _ from God.

However, God never stops l _ _ _ _ _ _ us.

If we return to Him, He will always w _ _ _ _ _ _ and f _ _ _ _ _ _ us.

Colour in this drawing of the prodigal son. You might want to write below what you imagine the prodigal son must have been thinking as he sat there with the pigs.

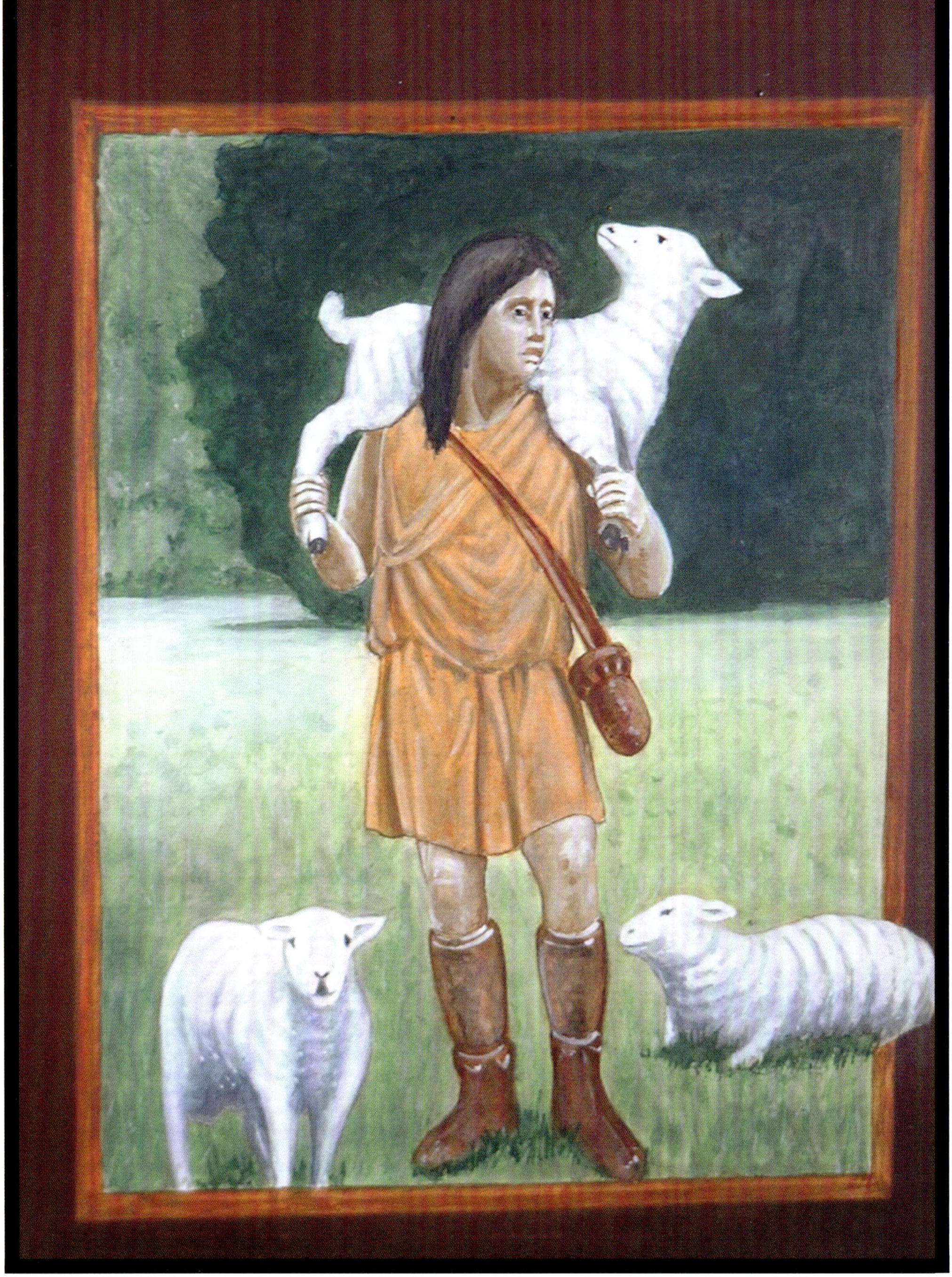

7. THE GOOD SHEPHERD

In the last lesson we saw how God our loving Father always forgives sinners when they turn back to Him. When Jesus was living on this earth He brought peace and forgiveness to those who lived in the sadness of sin. He loved to search for them as a shepherd looks for sheep who have wandered off, to bring them back to safety. He called Himself the *Good Shepherd* who never stops caring for and looking after the sheep, especially the silly ones who run away and put themselves in danger.

Before He returned to His Father in Heaven, Jesus gave His disciples, the first bishops and priests, the power to continue His marvellous work of bringing forgiveness to those who were sorry for their sins. On the evening of the day He rose from the dead, on the first Easter Sunday, He showed Himself to His disciples who had locked themselves into the Upper Room where, a few days before, they had eaten the Last Supper together. His first words to them were *Peace be with you.* And then He breathed on them and said: *Receive the Holy Spirit. Whose sins you forgive, they are forgiven.* This is how He gave them His power to forgive sins, and those disciples have, in their turn, handed on that power to the bishops and priests who have followed them. In this way Jesus continues His work of forgiving sins in our world today. In some countries the priest is called a *pastor*, which is Latin for *shepherd*. A bishop sometimes carries something called a crozier: it looks like a shepherd's crook, and reminds us that priests and especially bishops care for the flock of Christ. We are all members of that flock, and Christ is our Good Shepherd.

Bishops and priests use the power and authority Jesus gave them to take sins away in the Sacrament of Penance, also called confession. This sacrament is sometimes called the

Sacrament of Reconciliation, or the Sacrament of Pardon and Peace. When we go to confession Jesus forgives our sins, and increases His grace in us. This is why we should love to meet Him in this sacrament, so that, like the prodigal son, we can come closer and closer to God our Father and share more and more in his love and happiness.

When we are sorry for our sins and go to confession, Jesus, working through one of His priests, forgives our sins. Usually we go to confession in a special small room called a *confessional*. First we have to examine our conscience, to see what sins we need to confess. God has given each one of us a conscience, which is like a little voice inside us which tells us when we have done something wrong or something right. When we have checked our conscience we then ask God to help us to be sorry for our sins, and also to help us not to do them again in the future. When we are ready we tell our sins to the priest, who will give us some help and advice as well as something called our *penance*. The *penance* is usually a prayer or some prayers, or sometimes something for us to do, to show God that we are sorry for our sins and grateful for His forgiveness. After the priest has told us what our penance is God takes away our sins as the priest says: *I absolve you from your sins: in the name of the Father, and of the Son, and of the Holy Spirit.*

KEY WORDS FOR CHAPTER 7

Bishop
Sacrament
Penance
Confession
Confessional
Conscience
Absolve

Fill in the blanks

Jesus called Himself the
G _ _ _ S _ _ _ _ _ _ _.

Jesus gave His disciples the power to forgive sins. The disciples handed that special power and duty to the bishops and priests who came after them.

What is the name of our Holy Father the Pope? ....

What is the name of your bishop?..

What is the name of your pastor or parish priest?............................

In the parable of the Good Shepherd Jesus says: *Rejoice with me, because I have found the sheep that was lost.* Always remember that going to confession not only makes us happy, it makes Jesus and the angels and saints happy too. Colour in this picture of Jesus the Good Shepherd rescuing a lost sheep. This is what Jesus does when He helps someone in confession.

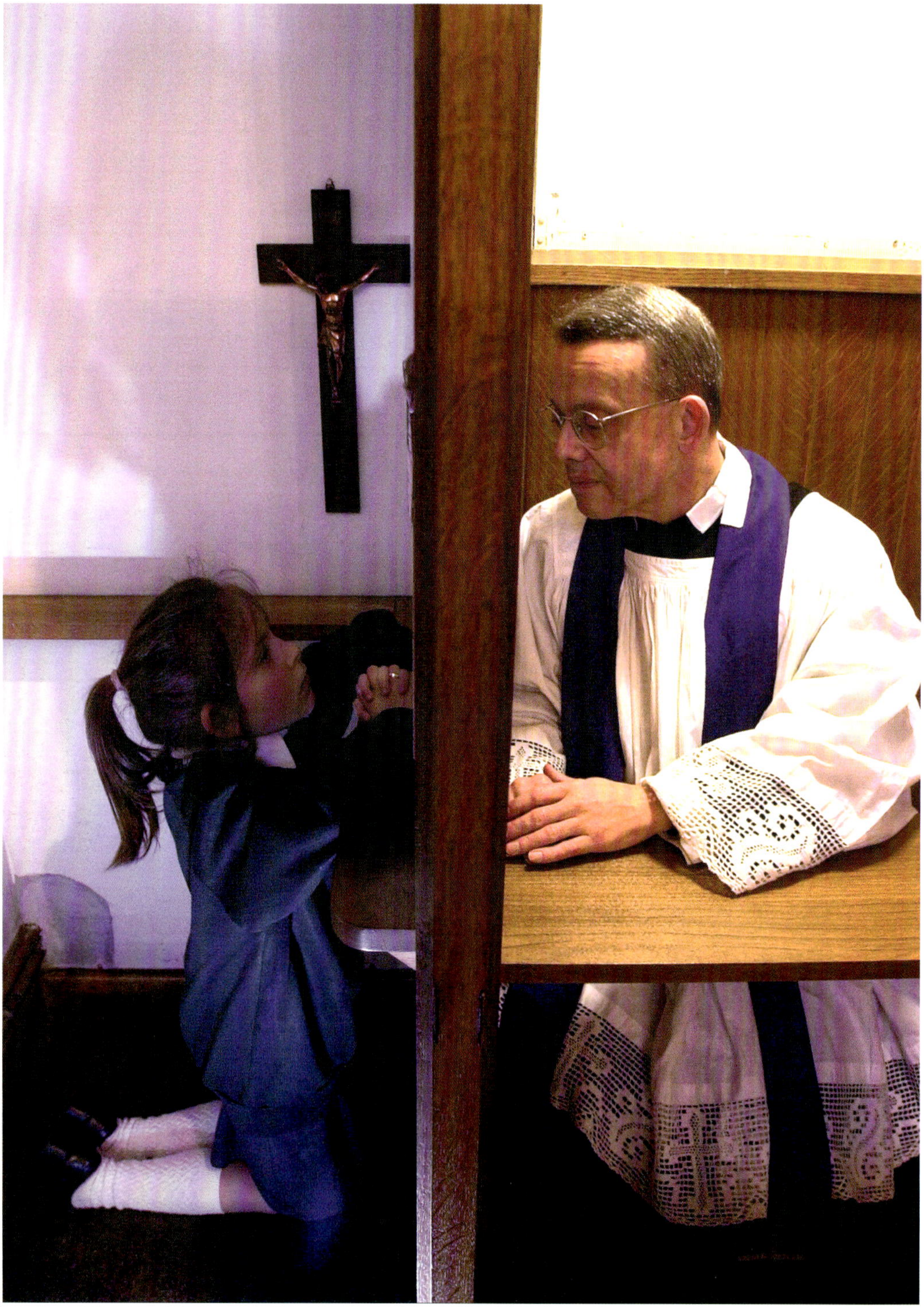

8. MEETING JESUS IN CONFESSION

Soon you will be making your first confession. *Confession* is the word people often use to mean the Sacrament of Penance. For most people this is the second sacrament they receive (Baptism was the first). We can only be baptised once, but we can and should receive the Sacrament of Penance as often as we need to. In this lesson we will learn how to prepare to meet Jesus in the sacrament of His forgiveness. Sometimes people ask how often they should go to confession. The answer to this is that they should go as often as they need to be forgiven! However, it is a good idea to go to confession at important times during the year: for example, at the start of Lent, and at Easter; for Christmas and other great feats like the Assumption (15 August) or All Saints (1 November). Many grown ups like to go to confession about once every month.

The first thing we need to do is to find out what sins we have to confess, and we do this by making an examination of conscience. It is good to examine our conscience every day, but we need to do so in a special way before we go to confession. We should ask God to help us know what sins we have committed. The following list of questions might help us know when we need to say sorry:

Have I said my prayers every day?
Have I used God's name in a wrong way?
Have I missed Mass on Sundays or holidays through my own fault?
Have I misbehaved at Mass?
Have I disobeyed my parents or my teachers?
Have I hurt others or been unkind to anyone at home or school?
Have I thought or done bad things, or said bad words?
Have I stolen anything?
Have I borrowed things, and not

looked after them or not given them back?
Have I cheated?
Have I told lies?

We can use a list like this, or make up our own, or use one we have found in a prayer book. After we have decided what we need to say, the next stage is to ask God to help us to be sorry for the things that we have done wrong. Anyone can just give a list of things that they have done wrong: to go to confession means that we are *sorry* for our sins. So we ask God to help us to be truly sorry.

The next stage is to ask God to give us His help not to sin again. When we go to confession we are not only saying sorry for what we have done wrong, we also promise God that we will try very hard not to fall into our sins again. Now we are ready to go to confession and to tell our sins to the priest. As we kneel down in the confessional we let Father know we are there by saying *Bless me Father, for I have sinned.* Then we tell him how long it has been since our last confession. When we make our very first confession we say *This is my first confession.* After our first confession we say *It is (however long since our last confession; for example four weeks, or two months) since my last confession.* Then we say what sins we remember that we have committed in that time.

The priest will then usually give us some help and advice. He will then tell us what penance we must do when we leave the confessional. As we saw in the last lesson, this will mean saying some prayers or perhaps doing something to help others. Then the priest asks up to show we are sorry for what we have done by saying a special prayer called the Act of Contrition. *Contrition* is another word for *Sorrow*. This does not mean that when we go to confession we should be unhappy and sad! Confession is there to make us happy and joyful. We should be sorry that we have done wrong, and happy that our Father in Heaven loves us and will help us do better. The Act of Contrition is a prayer that shows we are really sorry for our sins and that we really mean not to do those sins again in the future. There are many different ways of making an Act of Contrition. Here is one we could learn by heart:

> *O my God, because you are so good,*
> *I am very sorry that I have sinned against you*
> *And, with the help of your grace,*
> *I will not sin again.*

After this the priest gives us *Absolution*: this is the wonderful moment when God takes our sins away. The priest raises his right hand and says a prayer which ends, as we have seen, with the words *I absolve you from your sins, in the name of the Father, and of the Son, and of the Holy Spirit.* We then leave the confessional and say (or do) the penance given to us by the priest.

KEY WORDS FOR CHAPTER 8

Contrition

Absolution

Fill in the blanks

Before we go to confession we need to examine our c _ _ _ _ _ _ _ _ _; we need to be s _ _ _ _ for our sins. The prayer we use to tell God that we are truly sorry is called the Act of C _ _ _ _ _ _ _ _.

In the Sacrament of Penance Jesus takes away our sins when the priest gives us A _ _ _ _ _ _ _ _ _.

Copy out and learn by heart the Act of Contrition. You can use the one found in this chapter, or another one if you like.

9. HOW TO GO TO CONFESSION

When we go to confession we tell our sins to the priest, but we are really speaking to Jesus. The priest is a sort of telephone: taking our words to God, and giving God's message of forgiveness back to us. A telephone is an instrument to help people talk to each other, and, in confession, the priest is an instrument of God's mercy and forgiveness, taking our words to God, and giving God's love and blessing back to us. The priest is *never* allowed to tell anyone what he has heard in confession. Some priests have had to allow themselves to be killed rather than tell a word of what they heard in confession. We can be sure that anything we say in confession is private: we speak to God our loving Father, and He forgives us and brings us closer to Him.

In the last chapter we learnt about what happens when we go to confession. Here is a reminder of the five stages of a good confession. Before we go to confession for the first time we should learn exactly what we have to say and do, so that we can meet Jesus in this wonderful sacrament of His forgiveness.

1. Know your sins.
2. Be sorry for your sins.
3. Make up your mind never to commit them again.
4. Tell your sins to a priest.
5. Say or do the penance the priest gives you.

GOING TO CONFESSION

1. When you go into the confessional say: **Bless me, Father, for I have sinned. This is my first confession.** Or, when you next go, say: **Bless me Father, for I have sinned. It is (*say how many months or weeks*) since my last confession.**

2. Then you say your sins.

3. After this the priest will give you a penance to do to show that you are sorry. The penance will usually be a prayer for you to say after confession.

4. The priest will then ask you to tell God that you are sorry for your sins and will try to be better in the future by saying the Act of Contrition:

   O my God, because you are so good,
   I am very sorry that I have sinned against you
   And, with the help of your grace,
   I will not sin again.

5. The priest then gives Absolution, which is when God takes our sins away.

6. Leave the confessional and kneel down in the church, and say your penance.

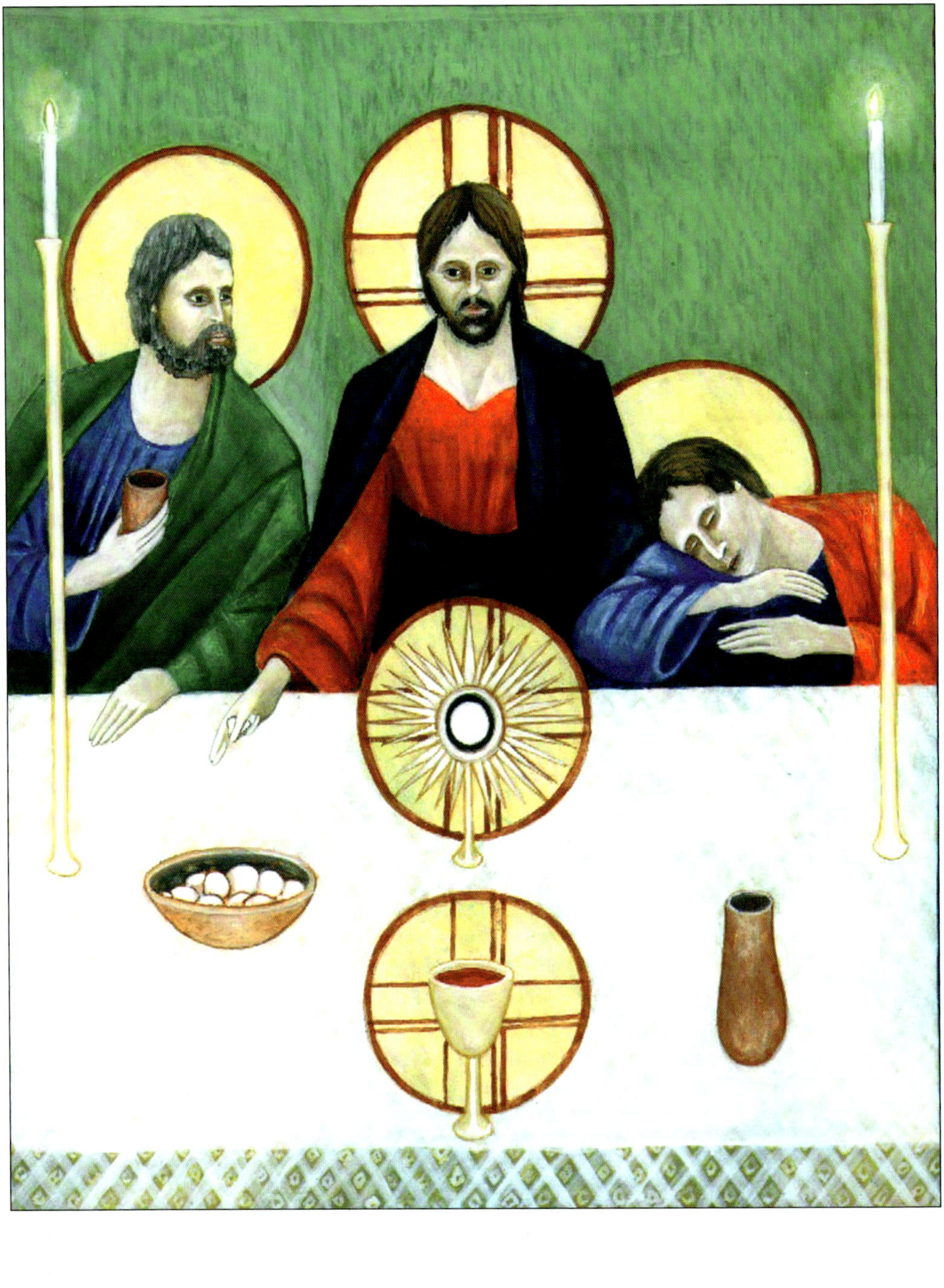

10. THE BREAD OF LIFE

We have already mentioned the Upper Room in the old city of Jerusalem. It was there that Jesus appeared to His disciples on the evening of the day He rose from the dead, and gave them the power to forgive sins in His name. This was the same room in which Jesus ate His last supper with the twelve apostles.

The Last Supper was always going to be a very important meal, since it was held on the night before Jesus died on the Cross. The disciples had prepared the Passover meal, which is a supper during which the Jews remember how God once saved their people from Pharaoh the King of Egypt, and led them out of slavery through the desert to the Promised Land. But this Last Supper was more than just another Passover. While they were all at table, Jesus took the special bread used for the Passover: this bread, like the bread we use for Mass, was flat because it was made without yeast. This sort of bread is called *unleavened bread*. Jesus took the bread, and blessed it. Then He broke it and handed it to His disciples and said to them 'Take this, all of you, and eat it, for this is my Body.' In the same way He took the chalice, the large cup used for the Passover. Again He blessed this, handed it to His Disciples and told them 'This is my Blood, the Blood of the new and everlasting covenant ...' With these words the Passover ended, and the Mass began. For the first time Jesus fed His people with His Body and Blood. This was the first Communion, the first Mass.

How could the disciples understand what Jesus was saying? What did He mean by saying *This is my Body* and *This is my Blood*? The Last Supper may have been the first time Jesus gave His Body and Blood to His disciples, but it was not the first time He had taught them about what He was going to do. At the synagogue, a place where Jews go to pray, in the town of

Capernaum, Jesus told the people that He was the Bread of Life, and that He would give His followers His Body to eat and His Blood to drink. When the people heard this, they could not understand how Jesus could do this. Many thought that the very idea was so horrible that they stopped following Him and went away. But Jesus did not change His teaching, even though many found it so hard to understand and accept. He told them that He was the Bread from Heaven, the Bread of Life.

It was at the Last Supper that Jesus showed how it was possible to give His people His Body to eat and His Blood to drink. The twelve apostles saw Him change the bread and wine into His Body and Blood: they heard for the first time the words said in every Mass: *This is my Body ... This is my Blood*. Not only did they see this: they also ate and drank: they received Holy Communion.

But Jesus did not want to give this wonderful gift of Himself only to His closest fiends. So, as He gave them His Body and Blood He also told them: *Do this in memory of me.* In other words He told the apostles, the first priests, to copy what He had just done for them. They did this, and we call this *the Mass*. At every Mass the priest says those words first heard in the Upper Room nearly two thousand years ago: *This is my Body ... This is my Blood.* And, as the priest says these words, Jesus is there, just as He was with His disciples at the first Mass, during the Last Supper.

KEY WORDS FOR CHAPTER 10

The Last Supper
Passover
Pharaoh
Yeast
Unleavened Bread
Synagogue

Fill in the blanks

On the evening before He died for us, Jesus ate a L _ _ _ S _ _ _ _ _ with His disciples.

At the Last Supper Jesus took bread, blessed it, broke it and gave it to His disciples and said 'This is my B _ _ _'. At the end of the Passover Meal He took the chalice and said 'This is my B _ _ _ _'.

Many famous artists have painted pictures of the Last Supper. Try to paint one below, making sure that you show the Bread and the Chalice on the table. The picture for this chapter might give you some ideas.

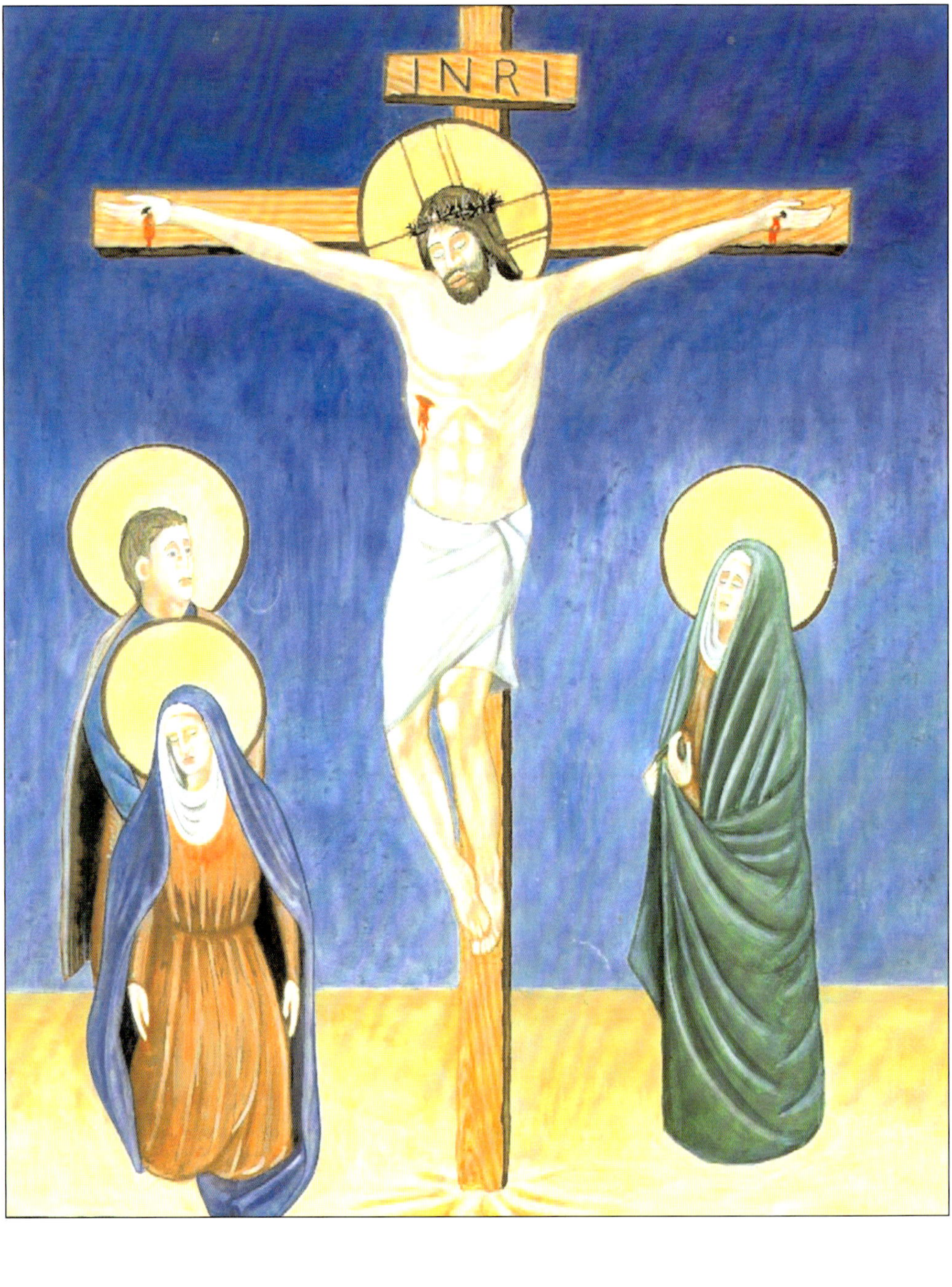
INRI

11. THE SACRIFICE OF JESUS

When we go to Mass there are many things to remind us of the Last Supper and the Upper Room. On the altar there are candles and fine white cloths: the sort of things people still use for a very important meal. The altar looks like a table: this reminds us that the first Mass took place during a meal, or rather during a banquet. A banquet is a special, important meal. Even the clothes the priests wears should remind us of the Last Supper: his clothes, called vestments, are based on the sort of clothes Jesus Himself wore at the Last Supper.

However, when we go to Mass there is something on or over the altar that certainly was not there at the Last Supper. This is a crucifix: a reminder of how Jesus died for us on Good Friday. Why is the Cross there on the altar? Why do we call the Mass a *sacrifice*?

We find the answer to this once again in those wonderful words of Jesus at the Last Supper. When He broke the Bread and gave it to His disciples, not only did He tell them *This is My Body,* but He added *which will be given up for you.* When He gave them the chalice and said *This is my Blood*, He also added *which will be shed for you.* Now, His Body was not given up as a sacrifice, nor was His Blood shed at the Last Supper in the Upper Room. Both these things happened the next day, on Good Friday, when Jesus was crucified on Calvary. So, as He celebrated the first Mass, Jesus was talking about what would happen the next day; about the sacrifice He would offer on the Cross. A sacrifice is a gift offered with love to God our Father. The greatest gift we can give anyone is our life itself. Jesus sacrificed His life for us on the Cross.

This is why we always see a crucifix at Mass. It reminds us that the Mass takes us not only to the Upper Room, but also to Calvary, where Jesus died for us on Good Friday. The altar and the crucifix remind us that the Mass is a banquet and also a sacrifice: the greatest, the most perfect sacrifice, the gift of Himself that Jesus offered to His Father on the altar of the Cross. Just as the disobedience of Adam and Eve at the tree of the knowledge of good and evil brought sin and sadness into the world, so the obedience of Jesus on the tree of the Cross destroyed the power of sin and brought grace and joy back to the world. Every time we come to Mass we are present at that great sacrifice, when peace and joy returned to the earth. Over the centuries Catholics have sometimes had to make great sacrifices to be present at Holy Mass: sometimes risking their lives or walking great distances – in some countries, this still happens, even today. It is a privilege as well as a joy for us to go to Mass.

KEY WORDS FOR CHAPTER 11

Banquet
Altar
Crucifix
Sacrifice
Calvary

Fill in the blanks

The special clothes a priest wears at Mass are called v _ _ _ _ _ _ _ _.

Jesus died for us on G _ _ _ F _ _ _ _ _.

We call the Mass a s _ _ _ _ _ _ _ _ because, during Mass, Jesus offers Himself to His Father, as He did on the Cross on Calvary.

This is a drawing of a chasuble, one of the special vestments a priest wears when celebrating Mass. This chasuble has a cross drawn on it, to remind us that the sacrifice of the Mass and the sacrifice of the Cross are the same. Colour in this chasuble, and remember to choose for the background one of the colours used at Mass (white, gold, green, black, violet, rose or red).

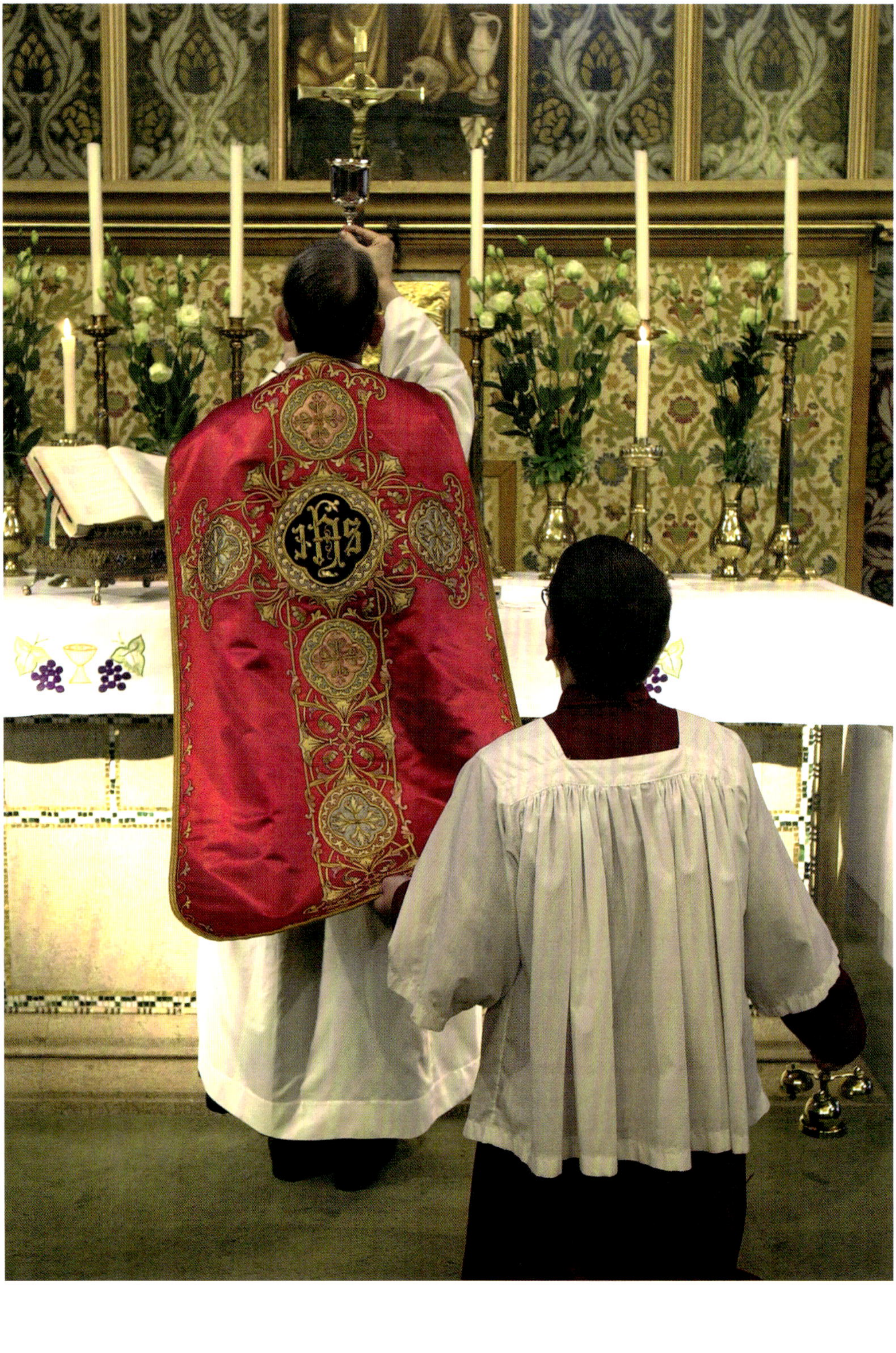

12. JESUS — GOD WITH US

When we pray we speak to God our loving Father. Jesus taught His friends a special prayer we call the *Lord's Prayer* or the *Our Father*. The Bible contains many other prayers, and holy people in the Church over the centuries have written many beautiful prayers used by Christians today. We should pray every day, but especially on Sunday when we come to Holy Mass.

The Mass is the greatest prayer of all because it is the prayer of Jesus Himself. In fact it is, as we have seen, the Sacrifice of Jesus Himself. In the Mass Jesus our Saviour becomes really present among us, and offers Himself for us to His Father. This happens at the part of the Mass called the *Consecration* – the most important moment in the Mass.

The Consecration takes place when the priest, taking the part of Jesus Himself, takes the bread, and, bending over it, says the words that Jesus used at the Last Supper: *This is my Body*. When he has said this he kneels to adore: because it is no longer bread, but the Body of Jesus! Jesus said *This is my Body*, and, since Jesus cannot tell a lie, we know that what the priest holds in his hands is what Jesus says it is: the Body of Jesus Christ given for us. The Host still looks like bread; in fact, it still tastes like bread: but these are only what it *appears* to be. It is no longer bread, it is Jesus, the Bread of Life.

Then the priest picks up the chalice, and repeats over it the words Jesus used at the Last Supper: *This is my Blood*. The wine in the chalice becomes Jesus: His Precious Blood shed for us. It still looks like wine, it tastes and smells like wine: but it is the Blood of Christ, poured out for us. The priest kneels to adore, because God is there. The altar servers ring the bells: to let us know that the most important part of the Mass is taking place, and to welcome Jesus with a joyful sound. At some Masses the servers also burn something called incense in a special metal container called a *thurible*. This makes a sweet-smelling smoke that rises up towards Heaven. For thousands of years people have burned incense to praise and adore God. We too should adore Jesus, our Saviour and our God at the Consecration, and repeat in our hearts the words of St Thomas the Apostle, *My Lord and My God!*

At the Consecration Jesus is really there on the altar: the bread and wine change into the Body, Blood, Soul and Divinity of Jesus Christ. (The word *Divinity* remind us that Jesus is God.) The appearance of bread and wine remains, but the bread and wine have gone: only Jesus is there. This change is called by a long and difficult word – one of the longest words in the English language: transubstantiation. This difficult word simply means that at the Consecration the bread and wine become Jesus: what now appears to be bread and wine is really the whole of Christ our Lord. It is a way of saying that when Jesus said *This is my Body* and *This is my Blood* He was telling the truth!

At the Consecration Jesus becomes present and offers Himself to His Father, just as He did at the Last Supper and on the Cross on Good Friday. Look at the candles and the cloths on the altar in the picture for this lesson; see the crucifix over it: they all remind us that as we kneel at the Consecration we are present in the Upper Room on Maundy Thursday, and at the foot of the Cross on Good Friday.

When the angel Gabriel told Mary that she had been chosen to be the Mother of Jesus, he told her that Jesus would be called *Emmanuel*: a name that means *God is with us*. At the Consecration at Holy Mass Jesus once more becomes Emmanuel: God with us. Come, let us adore Him!

KEY WORDS FOR CHAPTER 12

Consecration
Incense
Thurible
Divinity
Transubstantiation
Emmanuel

Fill in the blanks

The most important part of the Mass is called the
C _ _ _ _ _ _ _ _ _ _ _.

At the Consecration Jesus is really p _ _ _ _ _ _ and
o _ _ _ _ _ Himself to His Father.

During the Consecration the bread and wine become the B _ _ _ and B _ _ _ _, the S _ _ _ and D _ _ _ _ _ _ _ of Jesus Christ.

This is change is called T _ _ _ _ _ _ _ _ _ _ _ _ _ _ _ _ _.

Draw a picture of the altar of your church at the moment the Consecration takes place. You can show the priest and the servers, and also the Host or the chalice.

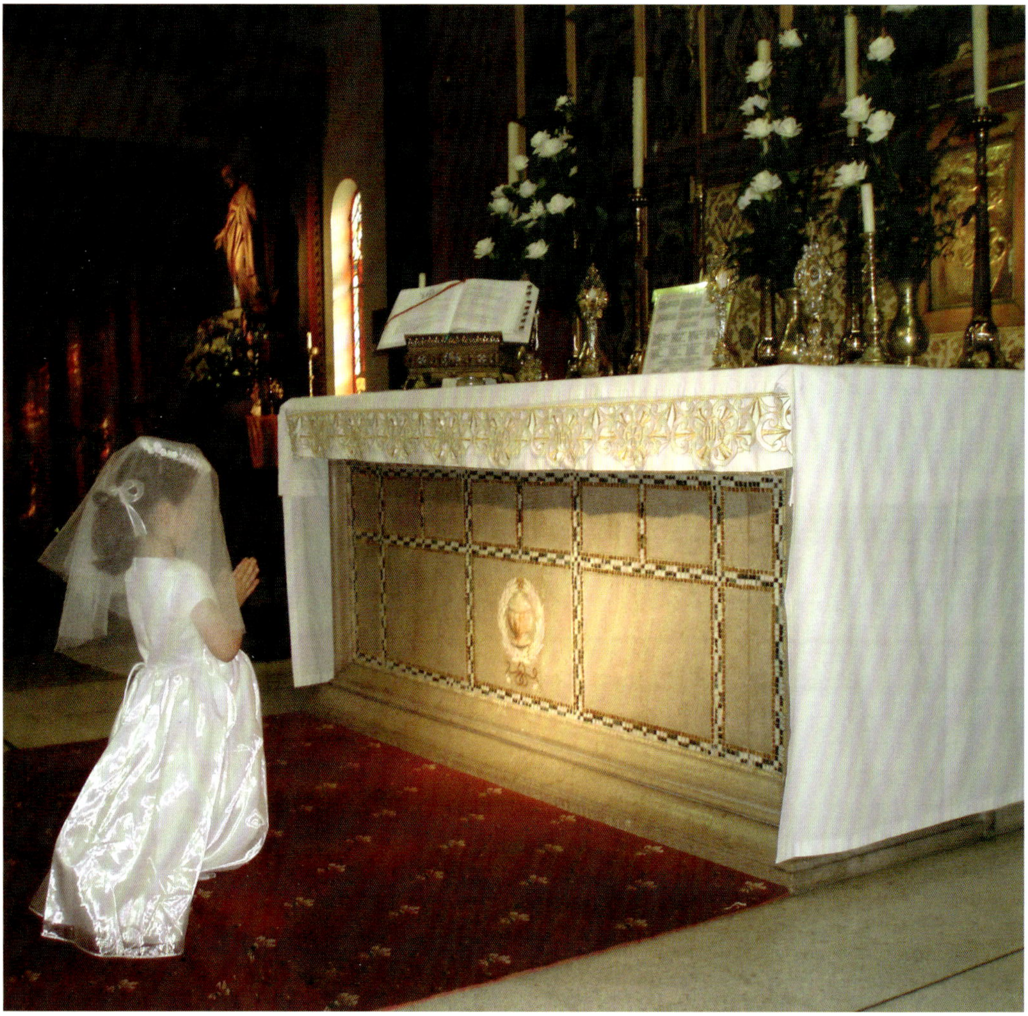

13. JESUS — OUR SAVIOUR AND OUR GUEST

In the last chapter we saw how, at the Consecration, during Holy Mass, the bread and wine become the Body, Blood, Soul and Divinity of Our Lord Jesus Christ. The Consecration takes place during a special prayer called the Canon or the Eucharistic Prayer. This important prayer is said by the priest: during this prayer he uses the words Jesus spoke at the Last Supper: *This is my Body*, *This is my Blood*, when, as we know, Jesus becomes really present and is offered to His Father in Heaven. You will find the words of the Canon or Eucharistic prayer in a missal, a book which contains the prayers for Holy Mass. Many people take missals to Mass with them, and there are special missals for children. In the missal you will find the words *This is my Body* and *This is my Blood* written in large letters, to remind us how important they are.

At the Last Supper, when Jesus had turned the bread and wine into His Body and Blood, He fed His disciples with this wonderful food: this was the first Holy Communion. The same thing happens at Mass. When the Eucharistic Prayer comes to an end, what prayer can we say, now that Jesus is really present on the altar? Only the prayer He Himself taught His disciples, the *Our Father*! When the *Our Father* or *Lord's Prayer* is over, the priest says some prayers, and then we sing or say the *Agnus Dei* which is Latin for *Lamb of God*. Saint John the Baptist first called Jesus the *Lamb of God*, the Holy One who would be offered up as a sacrifice for sinners. So now we pray: *Jesus, Lamb of God, have mercy on us*. Soon after this people start to go up towards the altar to receive Jesus in Holy Communion. In the picture for our lesson today you can see a little girl praying and waiting for Holy Communion: soon you too will be able to receive Jesus, the Bread of Life, in Holy Communion.

How should we prepare to receive Jesus in Holy Communion? The New Testament contains many accounts of Jesus visiting people in their homes. Once He was asked to cure the servant of a Roman centurion – a centurion was a soldier in the Roman army who had about one hundred men under his command. Jesus said that He would come and cure his servant, but the centurion spoke up: *Lord, I am not worthy to receive you under my roof; but only say a word and my servant will be healed!* Just before Holy Communion we repeat almost the same words the centurion spoke all those years ago, because, when we receive Holy Communion we too welcome Jesus 'under our roof': He comes to visit us, He makes His home in us. When someone important visits our school or our home, we make sure that everything is clean and in order: we tidy up and prepare carefully. No one is more important than Jesus Christ, so we need to prepare *very* carefully to welcome Him. Firstly, we must clean away the stain left by sin: Jesus gave us the perfect way to do this in the Sacrament of Penance or confession. We must also pay attention during Mass, just as we would if someone important came to our school or our home. When we receive Jesus we must make sure that we are at peace with others and never receive Holy Communion while thinking spiteful or unkind thoughts. Lastly, we should be fasting for one hour before Holy Communion. Fasting means that we eat and drink nothing (except water). People who are ill do not have to fast before Holy Communion, and taking medicines does not break our fast. Just before receiving Holy Communion we should tell Jesus that we love Him, and we should adore Him. Kneeling down or genuflecting is a good way of showing that we adore Jesus, Our Lord and Our God, Our Saviour and our guest, present in Holy Communion.

KEY WORDS FOR CHAPTER 13

Canon

Eucharistic Prayer

Missal

Agnus Dei

New Testament

Centurion

Fill in the blanks

The Consecration takes place during a special prayer called the C _ _ _ _ or the E _ _ _ _ _ _ _ _ _ _ Prayer.

Agnus Dei is Latin for L _ _ _ of G _ _.

The Roman centurion said to Jesus, 'Lord, I am not w _ _ _ _ _ to receive You'.

Before receiving Jesus in Holy Communion we must f _ _ _ for one hour.

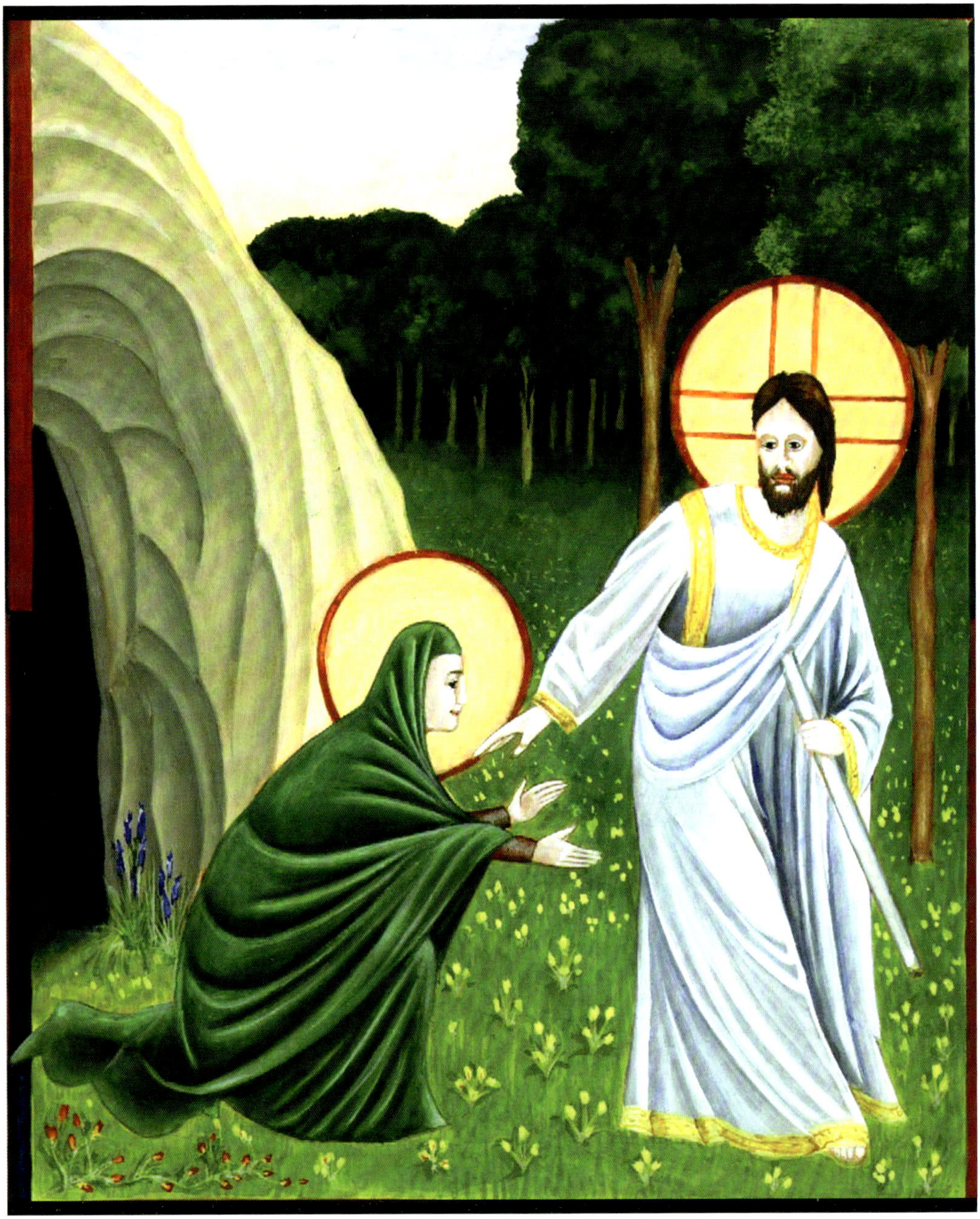

14. JESUS IS VERY NEAR

Very soon now you will receive Jesus for the first time in Holy Communion. There are probably all sorts of preparations for that great day going on right now in your family and in the parish. The First Communion girls may have been bought special dresses, and the boys new clothes. Perhaps there will be a party in the parish, or in your home after the First Communion Mass. Certainly, the church will be beautifully decorated for the First Communion: and people will be preparing the music, the decorations and the flowers.

All these things are important: they can help to make your First Communion day a day to remember all your life. But it is far more important to make sure that you are ready to receive Jesus, the Living Bread, into your soul in Holy Communion. In Holy Communion God Himself comes to visit us: this is so much more important than any party or special dress!

Before we can go to Communion, we need to know who it is who comes to us in the Host, in Holy Communion. That is why we have had all these lessons, so that we should learn how Jesus Himself comes to us in Holy Communion. We have seen that the Host we will receive is the Body and Blood, Soul and Divinity of Jesus Christ. We now know what Holy Communion is, and how much we should love and thank Jesus for this great gift of Himself!

The picture for our lesson shows Jesus on Easter morning, risen from the dead and leaving the tomb where He had been buried on Good Friday. With Him is Saint Mary Magdalene, the first person to see Jesus risen from the dead. When Mary Magdalene first saw Jesus there, in the Easter garden, she did not recognise Him; she thought He was the gardener. It was only when He called her by her name that she knew that it was really Jesus. Our lessons have taught us to recognise Jesus as He calls us to receive Him in Holy Communion.

In the last lesson we saw some of the ways we should prepare to welcome Jesus in Holy Communion. We should receive the Sacrament of Penance, that is, we should go to confession to make ourselves worthy to receive Jesus. Saint Mary Magadalene had committed many sins, but because she was sorry for them, because she loved Jesus so very much, she was the first of all His friends to greet Him when He rose from the dead. In the picture we see Mary Magadalene adoring Christ: her Saviour and her Friend, risen from the dead. During Mass we too should love and adore Jesus as we prepare to meet Him in Holy Communion. Here are some prayers we could say to help us prepare for our First Holy Communion. We can use these prayers not only to prepare for our First Holy Communion, but also every time we receive Our Lord in this wonderful Sacrament.

ACT OF FAITH

My Lord Jesus Christ, I believe that you are truly and really present in the Host, with your Body and Blood, Soul and Divinity. I believe this with all my heart, because you have said it, and your word is always true. I believe that in this Blessed Sacrament, you, my Saviour and my God will give yourself to me, to help me follow you and be more and more like you.

Jesus I believe in you: increase and strengthen my faith.

ACT OF CONTRITION

My dear Jesus, I am truly sorry for the sins I have committed. With the strength and the help I will receive from my Holy Communion, help me never to commit them again.

ACT OF LOVE

Lord Jesus Christ, you alone are my strength. You are the Living Bread come down from Heaven to be the food of my soul. I want very much to receive you in Holy

Communion. I am very happy when I think that you will soon come to me and live in me. Come, Lord Jesus; come and dwell in me, now and always! You love me so much; help me to love you with all my heart, and above all other things.

Holy Mary, Mother of Jesus, help me to receive your Son worthily. Saint Joseph and all the saints and holy angels, pray for me!

KEY WORDS FOR CHAPTER 14

Saint Mary Magdalene
Blessed Sacrament
Faith

Fill in the blanks

The Host we receive in Holy Communion is the B _ _ _, B _ _ _ _, S _ _ _ and D _ _ _ _ _ _ _ of Jesus Christ.

During Mass we should l _ _ _ and a _ _ _ _ Jesus as we prepare to receive Him.

In the box below write a prayer to Jesus, telling Him just how much you want to receive Him in Holy Communion. You can use words from the prayers in this lesson, or, better still, make up your own prayer.

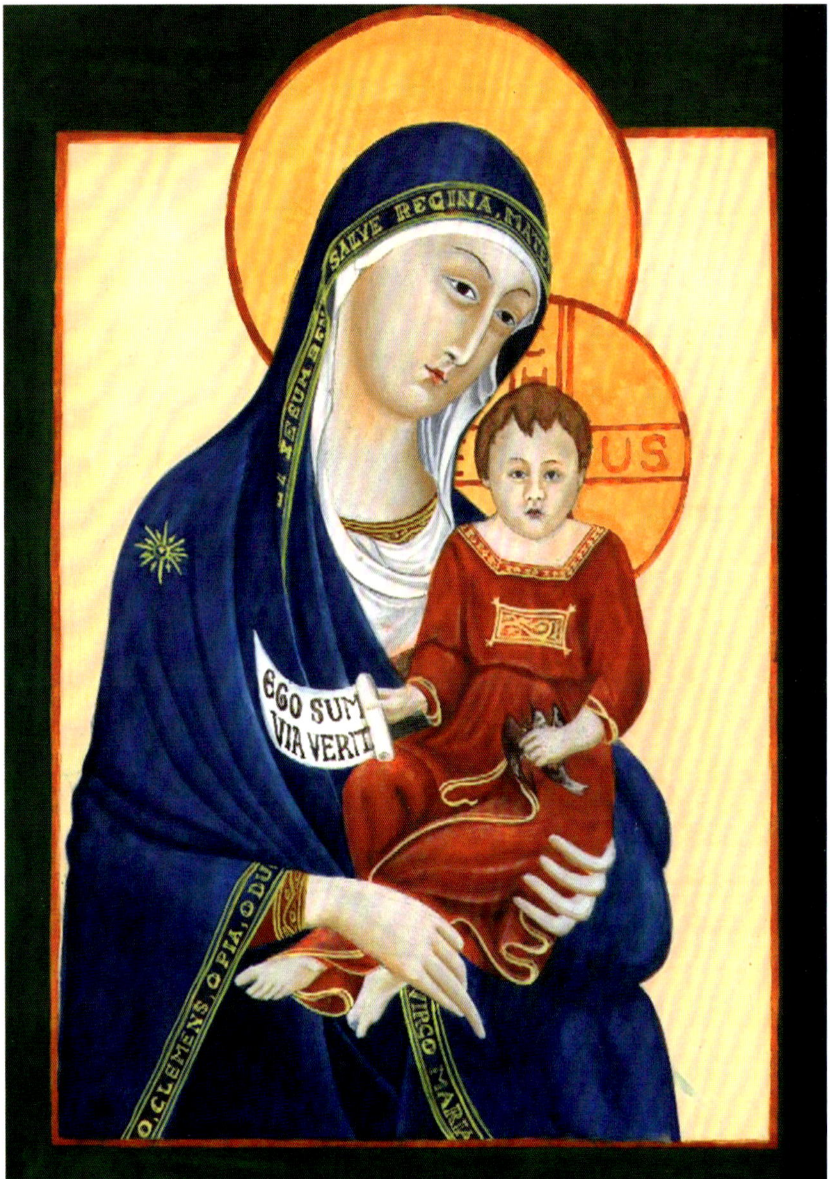
SALVE REGINA,
EGO SUM
VIA VERIT
O CLEMENS, O PIA,
VIRGO

15. IT IS RIGHT TO GIVE HIM THANKS

Your First Holy Communion will hopefully be the first of many meetings with Our Lord in the Blessed Sacrament. Over the last few weeks we have been learning how to receive Our Lord worthily in Holy Communion. In Holy Communion Jesus comes to us as our Saviour and also as our friend. We need to get to know Him in the Blessed Sacrament.

How do we get to know our friends? By spending time with them, of course! And it is the same with Jesus: to be His friend, we need to spend time with Him. We can do this when we come to church by spending time in prayer before the tabernacle where He awaits us in the Blessed Sacrament. (The tabernacle is the special place where any Hosts left over after Mass are kept, so that sick people who cannot get to Mass can be given Holy Communion, and so that Jesus will always be in our churches where people can visit Him. A lamp always burns near the tabernacle to tell us that Jesus in the Blessed Sacrament is there.) We genuflect to Jesus in the tabernacle before we take our place in church.

When we receive Holy Communion we become a sort of living tabernacle, a place where Jesus dwells. He only stays with us for a short while in this special way after Communion, and we must not waste this precious time. We call these moments after Holy Communion our *Thanksgiving*. During our *Thanksgiving* we should speak to Jesus: we can read special Thanksgiving Prayers, or speak to Jesus in our own words. We should tell Him how much we love Him, tell Him our needs and our worries, and listen to Him as He speaks to us. This is the time when we should get to know our Friend who loves us more than anyone else.

Never waste those wonderful moments after Holy Communion. When Jesus is with us we must give Him *all* our attention: there will be plenty of time to talk to our families and our friends once Mass is over and we have left the church. During our *Thanksgiving* we are like living tabernacles, carrying Jesus, the Living Bread from Heaven. Mary, His Mother was the first person to do this, and, as we prepare to receive Jesus in Holy Communion for the very first time, we should ask her prayers. The picture for our lesson today shows Mary carrying Jesus in her arms. No one knew Jesus better than Mary His Mother; no one loved Him better than Mary, and no one can help us to receive Him better than the Blessed Virgin Mary.

When Jesus was dying on the Cross He gave His Mother to be the Mother of all people. We ask her prayers for her children as they prepare to meet her Son Jesus Christ in Holy Communion. The best prayer to say to our Mother Mary is the *Hail Mary*. The first line of the Hail Mary contains the words the angel Gabriel said to Mary, when he was sent by God to ask her to be the Mother of His Son: 'Hail Mary, full of grace, the Lord is with thee!' The next line of this prayer is made up of words spoken by Mary's cousin Elizabeth. The angel Gabriel had told Mary that Elizabeth was soon to have a baby, and so Mary had set off to help her cousin. Saint Elizabeth was the mother of Saint John the Baptist, and Saint John, even though he was not yet born, leapt for joy when Mary came to see them. It was then that Elizabeth said the words we remember in the *Hail Mary*: 'Blessed art thou among women, and blessed is the fruit of thy womb!' *The fruit of thy womb* means Jesus. The last part of the prayer was written many years ago by holy people who wanted to ask the help and protection of the Mother of God.

As you prepare for Holy Communion, say the *Hail Mary* often, asking Mary our Mother to help you become a good and true friend of her Son, Jesus Christ. Have you noticed how good friends often become like each other? They get to like the same games; they like to dress in the same way; they learn special ways of talking, and special places they like to go. It is the same with Jesus: if we get to know Him in Holy Communion we will become more and more like Him every time we spend time with Him. Mary, our Mother and the Mother of Jesus, will help us become more and more like her Son, Jesus, the Living Bread from Heaven. Holy Mary, Mother of God, pray for us!

KEY WORDS FOR CHAPTER 15

Tabernacle
St Elizabeth
St John the Baptist

Fill in the blanks

The t _ _ _ _ _ _ _ _ _ is the special place where any Hosts left over after Mass are kept.

We call the moments after Holy Communion our
T _ _ _ _ _ _ _ _ _ _.

The best prayer to say to our Mother Mary is the H _ _ _   M _ _ _.

We can light candles when we come to church: they remind us to adore God and to ask the prayers of His Holy Mother and the angels and saints. Write a prayer to Mother Mary thanking her for her Son, Jesus Christ, the Bread of Life.

PRAYERS

The Lord's Prayer or *Our Father*

Our Father, who art in Heaven, hallowed be Thy name. Thy kingdom come; Thy will be done on earth as it is in Heaven. Give us this day our daily bread; and forgive us our trespasses as we forgive those who trespass against us; and lead us not into temptation, but deliver us from evil. *Amen.*

The Angelical Salutation or *Hail Mary*

Hail Mary, full of grace! the Lord is with thee: blessed art thou amongst women, and blessed is the fruit of thy womb, Jesus. Holy Mary, Mother of God, pray for us sinners, now and at the hour of our death. *Amen.*

Act of Contrition

O my God, because you are so good, I am very sorry that I have sinned against you; and, with the help of your grace, I will not sin again.

Grace before Meals

† Bless us, O Lord! and these Thy gifts, which we are about to receive from Thy bounty, through Christ our Lord. *Amen.*

Grace after Meals

† We give Thee thanks Almighty God, for these and all Thy benefits, who livest and reignest, world without end. *Amen.*

GLOSSARY OF KEY WORDS

(Note for parents and teachers: the following brief definitions describe the use of the words within the context of the relevant chapter – they are not intended to be exhaustive definitions.)

ABSOLUTION   The words the priest uses in confession by which our sins are forgiven.

ABSOLVE   To forgive sins (in confession).

ADORE   To worship God our loving Father.

ADAM AND EVE   The first human beings.

AGNUS DEI   Latin for Lamb of God.

ANGEL   A creature with no body: a pure spirit.

ALTAR   A table on which a sacrifice is offered, usually made of stone.

BANQUET   An important meal.

BAPTISM   The first of the seven Sacraments: it washes away sin and makes us children of God.

BETHLEHEM   The town in which Our Lord Jesus Christ was born.

BISHOP   A man who continues the Apostles' work of governing God's Holy Church.

BLESSED SACRAMENT   Jesus really present under the appearances of Bread and Wine.

BLESSED TRINITY   Three Divine Persons in one God.

CALVARY   The hill on which Jesus Christ was crucified for us.

CANON   The most important part of the Mass, during which the Consecration takes place.

CATHOLIC CHURCH   The Church Jesus Christ founded. The Head of the Church on earth is the Pope, also know as the Holy Father.

CENSUS   A great list of names of people and places.

CENTURION   A soldier in the Roman Army in command of a hundred men.

CONFESSION   A popular name for the Sacrament of Penance.

CONFESSIONAL   The small room in which confessions are heard.

CONSCIENCE   Is like a voice inside us that tells us if we have done right or wrong.

CONSECRATION   The moment at Holy Mass when the bread and wine become the Body and Blood of Jesus Christ.

CONTRITION   Sorrow for sin.

COVET   To desire, wrongfully, something that belongs to someone else.

CREATOR   God is the Maker of all things, visible and invisible.

CREATURE   Something, and especially *someone*, God has made.

CRUCIFIX   An image of Our Lord Jesus Christ attached to His Cross.

DEVIL   An evil spirit or wicked angel.

DIVINITY   *The Divinity of Christ* means that Jesus is God.

EMMANUEL   Hebrew word meaning God is with us.

EUCHARISTIC PRAYER   Another term for *The Canon of the Mass*.

FAITH   The virtue by which we believe in God and trust in what He has told us.

FOSTER FATHER   A man who takes the place of a child's real father.

FREE WILL   The gift men and angels have to serve God freely.

GENESIS   The first book of the Holy Bible.

GLORIA   A Latin word meaning Glory. The *Gloria* is often sung or said at Mass.

GRACE   The life and love of God dwelling in a person living in His friendship.

HOST   The special bread or wafer used at Mass which becomes the Body and Blood of Jesus.

INCENSE   A sweet-smelling dried gum burnt at Mass and other ceremonies.

INHERITANCE   Money or property given or left to an heir.

JOHN THE BAPTIST   The cousin of Our Lord who baptised Him in the river Jordan.

LAST SUPPER   The Passover meal Jesus ate with His disciples on Maundy Thursday.

LORD'S DAY   or Sabbath. Sunday, the day of rest from work.

MANNA   The bread from Heaven with which God fed His people in the desert.

MISSAL   The book that contains the text for Holy Mass.

MOSES   The leader of the Jews who took them from slavery in Egypt to the Promised Land.

NAZARETH   The town in which Jesus grew up.

NEW TESTAMENT   The second part of the Holy Bible, containing the four Gospels, the Acts of the Apostles, the Epistles and the Apocalypse.

ORIGINAL SIN   The first sin.

committed by Adam and Eve when they disobeyed God.

PARABLE   A story which contains a lesson.

PASSOVER   The yearly Jewish celebration of their escape from slavery in Egypt.

PENANCE   The sacrament by which sins committed after baptism are forgiven.

PHARAOH   The king of Egypt.

PRODIGAL   Extravagant or wasteful.

RIVER JORDAN   The river in the Holy Land where Jesus was baptised.

SACRAMENT   An outward sign of inward grace established by Jesus, by which grace is given to us.

SACRIFICE   Something offered up to Almighty God.

SAINT ELIZABETH   The cousin of the Blessed Virgin Mary and the mother of John the Baptist.

SAVIOUR   Our Lord Jesus Christ.

SYNAGOGUE   A place where Jews worship.

SIN   Disobedience to the will of Almighty God.

TABERNACLE   The place, in church, where the Blessed Sacrament is safely kept.

TEN COMMANDMENTS   Rules for living given by God to Moses on Mount Sinai.

TRANSUBSTANTIATION   The change of bread and wine into Christ's Body and Blood.

UNLEAVENED BREAD   Bread made without yeast.

YEAST   Something added to dough to make it rise.